SPOTLIGHT ON WEATHER AND NATURAL DISASTERS

EXPLORING EARTH'S WATER CYCLE

EMILY DONOVAN

PowerKiDS press.

New York

Published in 2019 by The Rosen Publishing Group, Inc.
29 East 21st Street, New York, NY 10010

Editor: Hannah Fields
Cover Design: Michael Flynn
Interior Layout: Tanya Dellaccio

Photo Credits: Cover Standret/Shutterstock.com; p. 5 artcasta/Shutterstock.com; p. 7 Merkushev Vasiliy/Shutterstock.com; p. 8 Ion George/Shutterstock.com; p. 9 Aleoks/Shutterstock.com; p. 11 (top) EddieHernandezPhotography/Shutterstock.com; p. 11 (bottom) chuckstock/Shutterstock.com; p. 12 Dmitry Polonskiy/Shutterstock.com; p. 13 Courtesy of the NOAA; p. 15 kazoka/Shutterstock.com; p. 16 Genova/Shutterstock.com; p. 17 Evgeny Bakharev/Shutterstock.com; p. 19 beboy/Shutterstock.com; p. 20 Courtesy of NASA; p. 21 Uriel Sinai/Getty Images News/Getty Images; p. 22 The Clay Machine Gun/Shutterstock.com.

Cataloging-in-Publication Data

Names: Donovan, Emily.
Title: Exploring Earth's water cycle / Emily Donovan.
Description: New York : PowerKids Press, 2019. | Series: Spotlight on weather and natural disasters | Includes glossary and index.
Identifiers: LCCN ISBN 9781508168980 (pbk.) | ISBN 9781508168966 (library bound) | ISBN 9781508168997 (6 pack)
Subjects: LCSH: Hydrologic cycle--Juvenile literature. | Water--Juvenile literature.
Classification: LCC GB662.3 D68 2019 | DDC 551.48--dc23

Manufactured in the United States of America

CPSIA Compliance Information: Batch #CS18PK For further information contact Rosen Publishing, New York, New York at 1-800-237-9932.

CONTENTS

CHAPTER ONE

WATER, WATER EVERYWHERE?

Water is one of the most important things on Earth. Plants, animals, and humans need water to live. Without water, life on Earth would end. Luckily, about 71 percent of Earth's surface is covered with water. This water is found in oceans, lakes, streams, and other waterways and areas across the planet. Some water on Earth is frozen into ice and snow, including huge ice mounds called glaciers. There's also water under the ground. This is called groundwater.

Though it sounds like Earth has a lot of water, 96.5 percent of all water on Earth is salt water. Humans and most animals can't drink salt water and most plants can't use it. Most of the life on Earth must share only a tiny part of all Earth's water in order to survive.

Water is an important **resource** for all life on Earth.

CHAPTER TWO

THE WATER CYCLE

If you have ever held a cold glass of water, splashed in the rain, or gone swimming, then you have experienced part of the water cycle. The water cycle is made up of three major parts: precipitation, evaporation, and **condensation**.

Precipitation is when water falls from the sky in some form. This water often ends up back in bodies of water such as oceans, lakes, and rivers. The water that falls on solid ground may flow back into these bodies.

The next step of the water cycle is evaporation. The sun warms the water on Earth. This turns some of the liquid into a gas. This water vapor rises from the surface of Earth into the sky.

As the water vapor rises into the **atmosphere**, it cools and changes to water droplets again through condensation. The droplets form clouds. They may then return to Earth as rain or other precipitation and the cycle continues.

Water moves around Earth in the water cycle. Earth has recycled the same water for years. This means that the dinosaurs drank the same water you do now!

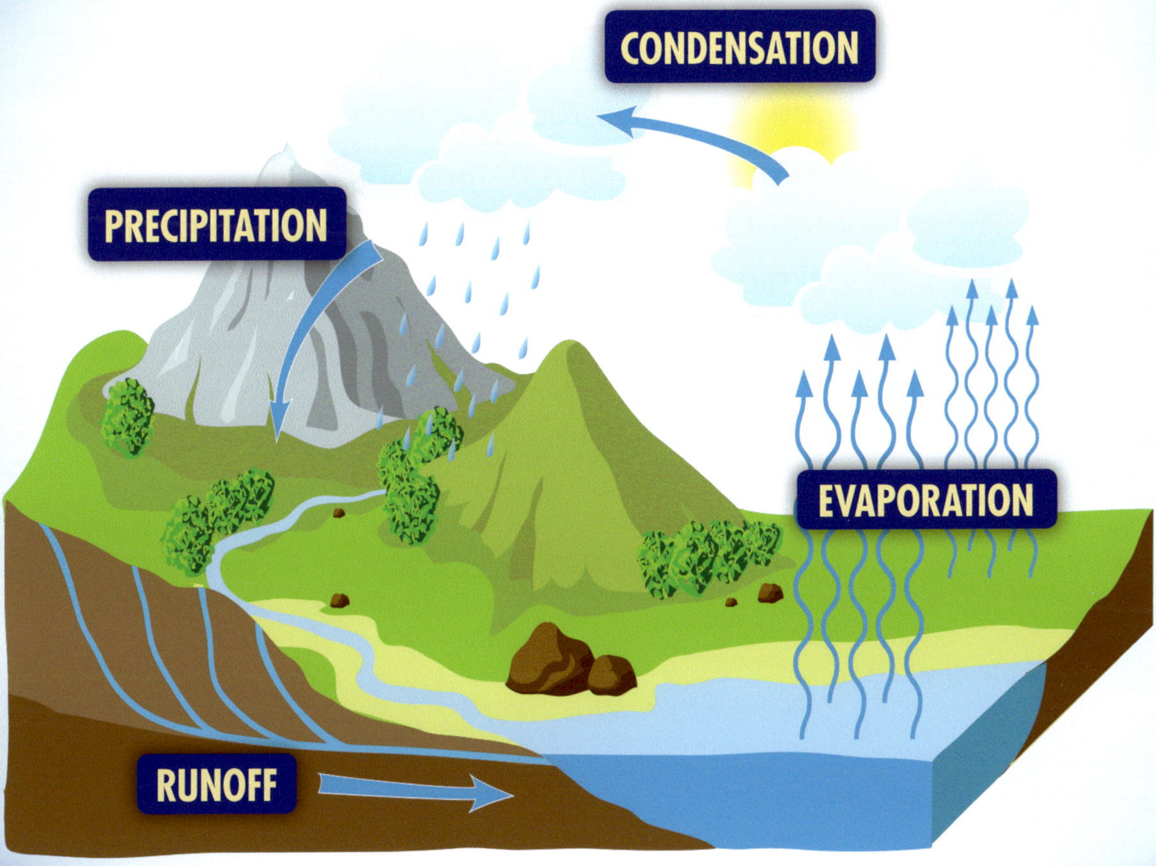

CHAPTER THREE

RAIN AND SLEET AND SNOW, OH MY!

Precipitation is most likely the part of the water cycle you know best. Precipitation happens when water falls from the clouds in the form of rain, snow, sleet, or hail. The temperature of the air **determines** what type of precipitation will fall.

HAIL

It can never be too cold to snow as long as there is moisture in the air!

If the temperature is warm, rain will fall. If the temperature of the atmosphere is below freezing, then ice crystals will form and the precipitation will be snow. Sleet is a mixture of rain and snow that forms when there's warm air high in the sky and cold air close to the ground. Hail is created when winds move water droplets high into the atmosphere, where it's colder. The droplets freeze into small pieces of ice. As they fall to Earth, the ice pieces may collect more water and get much bigger. Sometimes, a piece of hail can be as large as a golf ball!

CHAPTER FOUR

IT'S RAINING, IT'S POURING

Once a cloud can't hold more water, **gravity** pulls the precipitation down from the clouds. The water moves from the atmosphere to Earth's surface. Most precipitation falls to Earth as rain.

Precipitation does not fall on all parts of Earth equally. Most rain forests, which are warm and wet, get over 100 inches (254 cm) of rain each year. Deserts, which are dry, may get only 10 inches (25.4 cm) of rain each year. In comparison, the continental United States gets an average of about 30 inches (76.2 cm) of rain each year.

When a place doesn't get any precipitation for a long time, it goes through a drought. Droughts are dangerous because crops die, rivers dry up, and people may not have enough water. Droughts can cause fires and result in many deaths.

These pictures show Lake Tahoe in California during and after a drought.

CHAPTER FIVE

WHERE IS ALL THAT WATER STORED?

Water is found all over the world. It is stored in the clouds in the atmosphere, in oceans, lakes, streams, and other bodies of water, and inside living things like you.

Oceans store most of the Earth's water. In fact, they store 96.5 percent of the Earth's water. Only 2.5 percent

Glaciers and ice caps make up 68.7% of Earth's fresh water.

of the water on Earth is fresh water. While the oceans are important, people and animals will die without fresh water.

Most of the fresh water on Earth is frozen in glaciers and other ice. Some fresh water is groundwater. The water that you see most often in lakes and rivers is only a very small part of all the fresh water on Earth. This water is what keeps all the plants and animals on the planet alive.

CHAPTER SIX

HOT POTS AND WET LEAVES

Have you ever watched a pot of water come to a boil on the stove? As the water heats up, some of it turns into a gas. If the pot is heated for too long, it will run out of water.

On Earth, the sun acts like a stove. It heats the water on the planet and causes some of the water to turn into a gas. This gas, water vapor, rises into the air.

Plants go through a process called **transpiration**. This is when water moves through a plant and **evaporates** from the plant's leaves and other parts. Of all the water vapor in the atmosphere, 10 percent comes from transpiration.

The amount of water that evaporates from Earth's surface is almost the same amount that falls back down to Earth as precipitation. However, it can take Earth thousands of years to replenish its water supply, which is held in **aquifers**. If too much is used, Earth could run out of water just like the pot.

As warm water vapor rises out of a pot of boiling water, it meets cool air and condenses to form a cloud of steam.

CHAPTER SEVEN

HEAD IN THE CLOUDS

Imagine this: the day is hot and you decide to get a cool drink. After taking a sip, you look at your glass and notice the outside is all wet! As the warm water vapor in the air meets the cold glass, the water vapor cools and condenses to become liquid. This is the same process that forms clouds.

Clouds are created when water vapor moves up into the sky and cools. The vapor condenses and becomes a liquid. Clouds are very important because

Clouds can weigh as much as an airplane! Rising air that causes cloud formations keeps them floating in the air.

they produce precipitation so water returns to the surface of Earth. At night, clouds can also act as a blanket and keep part of the day's heat close to Earth's surface.

Condensation is also responsible for creating fog. Fog is just a cloud that's close to Earth's surface. Usually, fog is produced when warm air with a lot of water vapor in it meets the cold surface of Earth.

CHAPTER EIGHT

THE MOLDABLE EARTH

As water flows over the surface of Earth, it moves **sediment**. The sediment in the water hits the land and causes more earth to wear away. The wearing away of earth by wind or water is called erosion. Water is responsible for much of the erosion on Earth. Ocean coasts and the shores of waterways are always changing due to erosion.

Water that falls to Earth as precipitation soaks into the ground. It's stopped by solid rocks deep under the surface. This water moves slowly under the ground. Eventually, most of this groundwater makes its way back into bodies of water. There's actually 100 times more water under the ground than in all the rivers and lakes on Earth's surface.

Horseshoe Bend, which is part of the Colorado River in Arizona, is an example of how water wears at and changes Earth over time.

CHAPTER NINE

RAIN OF TERROR

Though rain and other forms of precipitation are very important to the water cycle, precipitation can also be dangerous.

Hurricanes are giant storms that form over the ocean. Their winds can move faster than 157 miles (252.7 km) per hour. That's faster than the world's fastest roller coaster! As a hurricane reaches the shore, the winds and rain it produces can lead to flooding, **destruction**, and even death.

Hurricane Harvey struck the United States in August 2017. The hurricane's winds reached speeds of 130 miles (209.2 km) per hour. It caused massive flooding in Texas and Louisiana.

Blizzards are another scary weather event. These are storms with winds stronger than 35 miles (56.3 km) per hour. They must cause visibility of less than a quarter mile (0.4 km) that lasts three hours or more. Snow is picked up by the wind and blown around, causing whiteouts. People can be trapped in their homes or cars for hours.

CHAPTER TEN

H2-OH-NO!

The amount of clean fresh water on our planet is shrinking. People and factories dump chemicals, plastic, and garbage into our water every day. This makes water sources unfit for drinking and also harms the plants and animals living near the water. People may not be able to swim in some bodies of water or catch fish there. The amount of **pollution** found in the water makes these activities unsafe.

There are many ways you can help prevent water pollution. You shouldn't pour paint or oil into your sink's drain or flush items such as baby wipes down the toilet. Cleaning up your dog's waste is also important. It keeps bacteria out of the **sewers** and water sources.

You may be only one person, but you can do a lot to help reduce water pollution and keep the water cycle healthy!

GLOSSARY

aquifer (AH-kwuh-fuhr) A layer of rock or sand that absorbs and holds water.

atmosphere (AT-muh-sfeer) The mixture of gases that surrounds a planet.

condensation (kahn-den-SAY-shuhn) The act or process of condensing, or changing from a gas to a liquid.

destruction (dih-STRUK-shun) Great damage or ruin.

determine (dih-TUHR-muhn) To officially decide something.

evaporate (ih-VAA-puh-rayt) To change from a liquid to a vapor.

gravity (GRAA-vuh-tee) The force that pulls objects toward the center of Earth.

pollution (puh-LOO-shuhn) The act of polluting, or making something unclean.

resource (REE-sors) Something that can be used.

sediment (SEH-duh-muhnt) Matter, such as rocks, sand, and stones, that's moved and deposited by water, wind, or glaciers.

sewer (SOO-uhr) A drain used to carry off water and waste.

transpiration (trans-puh-RAY-shuhn) The process by which plants give off water vapor through openings in their leaves.

INDEX

PRIMARY SOURCE LIST

Page 9
Icicles on the south side of a home illuminated on a bright winter morning. Photograph. Taken by Janet Ward. 2001. NOAA's National Weather Service (NWS) Collection.

Page 13
An iceberg in Gerlache Strait. Photograph. Taken by Rear Admiral Harley D. Nygren, NOAA Corps (ret.). March 1962. NOAA At The Ends of the Earth Collection.

Page 20
Hurricane Harvey, Seen From the Cupola of the International Space Station. Photograph. Taken by Jack Fischer. August, 25 2017.

WEBSITES

Due to the changing nature of Internet links, PowerKids Press has developed an online list of websites related to the subject of this book. This site is updated regularly. Please use this link to access the list: www.powerkidslinks.com/swnd/watcyc